POEMS

by

CONTEMPORARY WOMEN

POEMS

by

CONTEMPORARY
WOMEN

Compiled by
THEODORA ROSCOE
and
MARY WINTER WERE

With a foreword by
P. H. B. LYON, M.C., M.A.
(Headmaster of Rugby School, and author of
The Discovery of Poetry)

HUTCHINSON & CO. (Publishers), LTD.
LONDON :: NEW YORK :: MELBOURNE

FOREWORD

WAR, like all tragedy, brings us back to a truer sense of values ; we are 'purged by pity and terror' and see once more, beyond the darkened lights of our common paths, the glory of the stars.   It is for this reason, among others, that man has not rid himself of warfare; for he wearies of the shallows, and has not yet learnt to live intensely and dangerously in times of peace.   It is for this reason also that poetry, which speaks to and from hearts which are quickened to vigorous and painful life, must, in these days, wait for war-time before it can come into its own.

Anthologies are, in particular, welcome to the fighting man; for they offer him a varied excellence, poems for every mood and every taste.   There have been several in this war, though none perhaps to rank with the late Poet Laureate's *Spirit of Man*, which once again has found its way into many a soldier's knapsack as it did in 1917.   But here is a fresh claimant to favour, a chorus of voices, speaking to him not only of war, but of home, of the dreams of his heart and the ardours of his soul; songs to drown for a moment the urgent tumult into which he is thrust.   For the quieter the voice of the poet, the more powerful its spell; and the reader will find quiet voices here—'soft, gentle and low, an excellent thing in a woman'.

A man who is no poet may well feel embarrassed at being asked to play prologue to so gracious a company of muses; but he must feel honoured too.   It is indeed with a deep sense of privilege that I bid you give welcome to this little volume; may you find in it refreshment and delight.

HUGH LYON.

4

CONTENTS

Contents

ACKNOWLEDGMENT

Thanks are due to the following for permission to use the poems here enumerated:

To Joyce Grenfell and *The Times* for "Walford Davies" and "The Elms are Flowering", and to the *Observer* for her "At Night", "Summer in Wales" and "March Day, 1941"; to the *Spectator* and Diana James for her "Munition Workers", "Dallas: His Dirge" and "Führer"; to Marguerite Edgelow and the *Jongleur* for "English Pastoral"; to Marie Stopes and Messrs. Heinemann for "The Lift Descending" and "Instead of Tears"; to Susan D'Arcy Clark and the *Daily Telegraph* for "Dunkirk"; to Doreen C. Watts and the *Jongleur* for "Fragment"; to Carla Lanyon Lanyon and the *Jongleur* for "Into the midst of Battle"; to Mary Winter Were and the *Month* for "Heaven"; to Camilla Doyle and the *Jongleur* for "To the Blackbird in March"; to Beatrice Gibbs and *Country Life* for "Trout", the *Lady* for "Night", the *Sunday Times* for "The Bomber" and "Heritage"; to V. Sackville-West and Messrs. Heinemann for "Fritillaries"; to Messrs. Williams and Norgate and Lady Margaret Sackville for "Magnolia" and "Neglected Woods"; to V. H. Friedlaender and *Country Life* for "Trivial Detail"; to Margaret Stanley-Wrench and *Time and Tide* for "Legacy", to the *Lady* for "Autumn Roses" and "Ploughing up the Pasture", to Ada Jackson for "Widow-Mother", "Blessed Event", "Hitler Youth" and "I Have Seen England"; to Dorothy Wellesley for "The Buried Child"; to Margaret L. Woods and The Bodley Head for "March Thoughts from England".

These poems break new ground. Among the contributors' names are those unfamiliar as writers of poetry. May readers enjoy and ask for more of their work. Other names here are already well known.

7

We are happy to pay tribute to one of the greatest of our women poets, Margaret L. Woods, who has kindly permitted the inclusion of her poem "March Thoughts from England". Through her we have a link with the Victorian poets, for, as a child, she sometimes stayed at Farringford, and among the family circle listened to Tennyson reading his poems. Thus we have here represented some of our youngest women poets linking hands with one who, old in years and wisdom, has a spirit that never will grow old as she tells us in her *Guadeamus Igitur*:

> When at length the grasses cover
> Me, the world's unwearied lover,
> If regret
> Haunt me yet,
> It shall be for joys untasted,
> Nature lent and folly wasted.

T. R.
M. W. W.

BIOGRAPHICAL NOTES

EVELYN D. BANGAY lives at Chesham, Buckinghamshire. She has always been closely associated with the Poetry Society.

VERA BRITTAIN, M.A., is well known as a novelist. She served abroad as a V.A.D. in the last war (*Verses of a V.A.D.*) Her *Testament of Youth* brought her worthy recognition, as also did her *Testament of Friendship* (1940).

SUSAN D'ARCY CLARK lives in Derbyshire, where she interests herself in the musical life of the county. Besides writing poetry she has composed, and had published, eight songs since the war. All her children are serving in the war. A member of the Society of Women Journalists.

CLEMENCE DANE. Novelist, dramatist. Her best known works are: *Regiment of Women, Broome Stages* (novels), *A Bill of Divorcement, Will Shakespeare, Granite* (plays). These were followed by *The Saviours* and *The Cathedral Steps*, which express her love for the dramatic and for pageantry. She is the President of the Society of Women Journalists.

CAMILLA DOYLE lives in Norwich, her home town. She is a painter as well as poet. Studied painting at the Slade School and in Paris. Member of the Women's International Art Club. Published *Poems* (Basil Blackwell, 1923), *Poems* (Ernest Benn, 1927), *The General Shop and Other Poems* (St. Catherine's Press).

MARGUERITE EDGELOW (Mrs. Wykeham Edmonds) has had poems in the *Poetry Review* and other periodicals. She is a graduate of London University (Diploma in Journalism). Has had criticisms, articles and reviews in English and Canadian periodicals. Is teaching art, English, and history as a war job. Married to E. Wykeham Edmonds, author of

Versailles Summer, who is now in the Army Education Corps.

V. H. FRIEDLAENDER has written poetry, novels and essays, and has done much reviewing of poetry for *Country Life* and other periodicals. Her two books of poetry are *Mirrors and Angles* and *Friendship and Other Poems* (Country Life, Ltd.); her essays *Pied Piper Street* (Arrowsmith), and her novels *Mainspring* and *The Colour of Youth* (Collins and Putnam).

BEATRICE GIBBS was born and brought up in Devonshire. Her poems have appeared in many journals. She has written short stories and one book for children. Is a member of the Society of Women Journalists.

JOYCE GRENFELL. Born London. Mother from Virginia, U.S.A. Radio critic on the *Observer* 1936–39. Writes and acts character sketches. Writes songs with Richard Addinsell and sings them on the air.

BLANCHE HARDY has written historical biographies; the *Princesse de Lamballe*, *Arabella Stuart*, and historical novels; *Sanctuary*, *Dynasty*, *The Girl in the Red Gown*. Member of the Society of Women Journalists.

ADA JACKSON lives in Staffordshire. Her long poem "Behold the Jew" recently won the Greenwood Prize and was printed in the *Poetry Review*. America called her the Elizabeth Barrett Browning of our time, and E. V. Lucas named her the English Emily Dickinson.

DIANA JAMES is our youngest contributor, some of her work appearing in the *Spectator* when she was only fifteen and sixteen years old.

CARLA LANYON LANYON has had three books of poetry published. She is the wife of an Army officer and has three young children. She has travelled much, and for a time was stationed at Gibraltar, where her *Into the Midst of Battle* was written. She is a member of the Society of Women Journalists.

SYLVIA LYND (Mrs. Robert Lynd). Novelist and poet. Her book of poems, *The Goldfinches* (1920), and the volume in *Augustan Poets* (1928) are well known.

VIOLA MEYNELL, the daughter of the poet Alice Meynell, is a novelist, and has published one book of poetry. She has written a memoir of her mother, and has edited the *Letters of J. M. Barrie.*

MURIEL NEWTON has contributed poems to the *Observer*, the *Field*, *Poetry Review*, the *Adelphi*, and other periodicals. She is also a writer of short stories. Has done much work with the W.V.S. Now lives in the country; has two sons serving in the Forces.

RUTH PITTER had her first book of poems published in 1920. *A Trophy of Arms* won her the Hawthornden Prize in 1936. Her last book of poems, *The Rude Potato* (1941), was widely read.

THEODORA ROSCOE, M.R.S.L., is interested in painting as well as poetry. Has had three books of poems published. Contributed articles to the *Contemporary Review* ; *The Times* ; *Time and Tide.* Her husband is in the Army, and with him she travelled to many lands, including Australia, where she was most happy. She is the Hon. Secretary of the Society of Women Journalists. Lives in the country.

LADY MARGARET SACKVILLE, whose books of poetry are well known, has always been associated with the Poetry Society, where she presents yearly the Lady Margaret Gold Medal for poetry reading. Recently, as a tribute to her poetry and her many social activities, her bust by Dr. Macgillivray was purchased by public subscription and presented to the Scottish nation.

V. SACKVILLE-WEST (The Hon. Mrs. Harold Nicolson), whose novels are as well known as her poetry, lives in Kent, which county forms a background for much of her poetry, and for her literary work.

MARY DOREEN SPENDER, M.B.E., F.R.S.A. By profession a schoolmistress, Past President of London

Head Teachers' Association. First woman to be appointed head of a Senior Mixed School under the L.C.C. Awarded M.B.E. for work in education. Took great interest in swimming and life-saving. Has done much work in educational journalism and reviewing. Poems published in *Country Life*, *British Australasian*, and local and colonial papers. Represented in *London Pride* and *Wessex Anthology*, published by Fowler Wright, Ltd. At present in charge of evacuees in South Wales. Hobbies: wild flowers, music. Is the aunt of Richard Spender, the young poet who was killed in North Africa whilst serving with the Parachute Regiment.

MARGARET STANLEY-WRENCH, M.A. (Oxon). Won Newdigate Prize, 1937, with *The Man in the Moon*. Published book of poems *Newsreel and Other Poems* (1938). Wrote Prologue for Conference of the Associated Countrywomen of the World held in London, 1939. Now working in the Home Office. Has had poems published in periodicals here and in the U.S.A.

LOUISE STEWART is a member of the P.E.N. club. Was the first Scotswoman to fly the Alps as a passenger. Has written and lectured on Poland. Has published three books of poetry. Was elected an Hon. Member of the Caledonian United Service Club in recognition of her splendid war services, especially in connection with the Navy League. A writer of children's stories. A member of the Society of Women Journalists.

MARIE CARMICHAEL STOPES, D.Sc., has written much poetry besides her many books on the marriage question. Gardening is one of her recreations. A member of the Society of Women Journalists.

O. I. WARD has written mostly articles on archæological subjects and travel sketches. A member of the Society of Women Journalists.

DOREEN C. WATTS (Mrs. Simon Armetage) is a writer of children's short stories as well as of poetry. Her husband is now serving overseas in the Intelligence Department. A member of the Society of Women Journalists.

WELLINGTON, THE DUCHESS OF (Dorothy Wellesley), whose first book, *Poems*, was published in 1920, followed by *Genesis* in 1926, and recently *The Poets and Other Poems*, has generously encouraged the art of poetry. Her Poetry Readings arranged at Tunbridge Wells draw poets and poetry lovers to this centre.

MARY WINTER WERE (Mrs. Arthur Hughes) has published several books of poems, including *The Night He Came*, *The Gardener*, *His Roses and Other Legends of the Christ-Child*, *Peace-Music* (Samuel Bagster and Sons), *To-Morrow*, and *Cross and Shrine* (Sands and Co.). *Shepherds of Bethlehem*, a story of the Holy Land (Sands); and of a book of essays, *Things Worth While* (Samuel Bagster and Sons). Has contributed to the *Month*, the *Catholic Gazette*, *Poetry Review*, *Country Life*, *Chambers's Journal*, *British Weekly*, *Bookman*, the *Lady*, *Green Quarterly*, *Glasgow Evening Times*, *Occult Review* and *London Forum*. She is a collateral descendant of Robert Southey; for some years has represented Shortlands on the Council of the Poetry Society and is a member of the Society of Women Journalists. She has one daughter now serving with the A.T.S.

MARGARET L. WOODS is a member of the Academic Committee of the Royal Society of Literature. She is the daughter of the late G. G. Bradley, D.D., Dean of Westminster. She married the Rev. H. G. Woods, President of Trinity College, Oxford, who was later Master of the Temple. Her novels comprise *A Village Tragedy*, *Esther Vanhomrigh*, *A Poet's Youth*. Her first poems, *Lyrics and Ballads*, were published in 1889, and her *Collected Poems* in 1913.

Evelyn D. Bangay

THE FIRST AIR-RAID WARNING

When the quiet acres I look upon were shaken—
Not by a drum-pulse quickening the hand
But sinisterly, sourly, by factory sirens taken
Into the service of A.R.P.'s command—
Quietly the men there engaged in turnip-hoeing,
Glancing to skyward, weatherwise and calm,
Deftly continued to thin the farmer's sowing,
Saw the hurrying wardens and spat upon their palm.
 Would I had their wisdom and faith each waiting day . . .
  Not seed-time and harvest, but wars, shall pass away.

MOTHER AND CHILD
(*War Victims*)

We made room for you, remembering
The over-filled, inhospitable Inn,
With half the world now persecuted, homeless,
The ordered ways destroyed, and wars to win.

No gifts come, for kings are without their kingdom,
Necessity controls the shepherds' shears,
But you have brought your own wealth, all-providing
Of golden love, and innocence, and tears.

ON PLOUGHING

The slow shuttle of husbandry
Has plodded up and down
Till folds of tilth are lying
In ripples of shining brown.

14

The slow thoughts of my ancestry
Are moving across my brain,
Turning today's deeds under,
Laying the old facts plain:

How my father strode at his furrowing,
My mother's father spun
And worked in the mills of weaving;
So the image of both is one . . .

The plough, horses and harnessing
Weaving slow lines of thread:
My grandfather and my father
Sweating for daily bread.

Vera Brittain

BOAR'S HILL. OCTOBER, 1919

Tall slender beech trees, whispering, touched with fire,
Swaying at even beneath a desolate sky;
Smouldering embers aflame where the clouds hurry by
At the wind's desire.

Dark sombre woodlands, rain drenched by the scattering
    shower,
Spindle that quivers and drops its dim berries to earth,
Mourning, perhaps as I mourn here alone for the dearth
Of a happier hour.

Can you still see them, who always delighted to roam
Over the Hill where so often together we trod,
When winds of wild Autumn strewed summer's dead
    leaves on the sod,
Ere your steps turned home?

SEPTEMBER, 1939

The purple asters lift their heads
Beneath the azure Autumn skies;
Above the sunflower's golden cup
Hover the scarlet butterflies.

Not in the sandbagged city street
Where London's silver guardians soar,
But through the cottage garden throbs
The aching grief of England's war.

FAREWELL TO A LOVER

Your body was my temple
Wherein the pitiful ghosts of the Somme and Arras
Reclothed themselves in the warm pulsating vestments
Of uncorrupted flesh;
And the life, the life of the lovely dead re-awakened
When my captive desire
Turned aside to pursue the vagrant lure of your shadow.

Your body was my sepulchre,
Wherein the complacent whiteness of glory and honour
Burned away to a heap of grey spendthrift ashes
On the ultimate altar;
But the ghosts of the War shall walk for ever
By that grave of contentment
Where ripen the bitter-sweet fruits in Gethsemane's
    garden.

Susan D'Arcy Clark

DUNKIRK

They looked at Death,
And with him nonchalantly passed the time of day,
He paused bewildered—said beneath his breath
"Immortals these," and laid his scythe away.

SEARCHLIGHT

And now must every man his soul explore,
    Illumine any doubt, or craven fear,
These flood-lit and controlled, acclaim once more
    The Conqueror enrolled, braced to endure.

"GONE AWAY"

There are leathers and boots in the stable
    With a varied assortment of "tack";
A hunter, unclipped, in the meadow
    Waiting for "him" to come back.
But they ride over clouds, on wing'd horses
    Tally-Ho!   "Gone away"; with a drone,
No fox, but the Devil's own Forces
    The huntsman and pack hunt alone.

TOCCATA IN D MINOR (Bach)

Breakers insistent, massive, persistent—
    Thunder the grandeur of life;
Gaining momentum, starkly resistant,
    Nature unleashed—and at strife.

Unbaffled, receding, leaving a seaboard
    Tidewashed, but flooded with light;
Sighing, unheeding, weaving a D chord,
    Rollers—far out in the night.

PLYMOUTH

I've just been down to Plymouth.   Did you know
that lovely place before the trouble started?
Well, you'd be broken-hearted
if you could see it now, I tell you that,
The mess the 'planes have made!
Acres laid flat!
It's cruel—day and night, raid after raid!
And how the people stick it out, God knows!
I wouldn't know.

But there they are, and, stubborn, there they stay.
They work all day
between the bombs.   At night—this moved me most—
an hour before the sun goes down
they flock, the ruined people of the town,
to listen to the band,
(light music, nothing grand)
and dance, or watch the dancing, on the Hoe.

Who dance?   Oh—sailors—girls from a canteen—
men at a warden's post—
a smiling couple from a salvaged home—
or others who've lost everything.   They come
for company, to change their thoughts, to rest:
and shabby clothes don't matter on the Hoe.

The waters darken, purple dyes the west,
the hilltops lose their green,
the stars begin to glow.
Black-out!   As home they go
the 'planes are heard afar.

19

This was the second summer of the war;
yet every night, sedately,
most innocent and stately,
the boys and girls were dancing,
were dancing on the Hoe.
The boys and girls of Plymouth
were dancing on the Hoe.

THE WHITE OWL

He comes in the twilight—
Evening after evening;
Year after year we have watched him.

The last rays of the sun
Seem held in his transparent wings
Whose quills themselves are spread as glimmering rays.

He sweeps round the field
With dignity and mystery,
With the pride befitting a bird of legend,
As though he remembered that a goddess with an owl
Was worshipped in Ancient Greece.

He seems very old,
Old with the antiquity of shadowy barns,
The antiquity of hollow trees,
The antiquity of Night.

AT THE FIRE-FIGHTERS' POST

This was a stately Victorian drawing-room
Where ladies worked at tatting,
Resting on ottomans,
Sitting down sideways
To manage their crinolines gracefully.
Now by day it is an office
Filled with desks and typewriters

Quite unsuited to any room planned for leisure,
To any room adorned with moulded cornice,
With ornate fireplace;
And by night our beds, our lanterns, our helmets
Bring still more confusion,
Till that which had merely
Come down in the world
Grows as wild as a dream.

It was just as well, tranquil Victorian ladies,
That you, like all the folk of your period,
Prided yourselves on common-sense,
Disbelieved in the Second Sight,
Never consulted a seer to tell you the future,
Never guessed what lay in store for your home.

But also you never guessed
How happy you were.

A GAME OF BOWLS
(*Written During an Air Raid*)

My body's crouched beneath a "Table Shelter",
    But my unhampered mind is far away;
My hands may quiver and my breathing falter
    But still my memory watches men at play;
They played at bowls—I see the "woods" still rolling,
    And hear the gentle clinking when they touch;
I see the friendly smiles that greet good bowling;
    My shelter shakes, but I shan't mind too much
If only I can keep those bowlers playing
    Just as they played last month, beside a wall
Of sunlit yellow stone—yes, they are staying,
    I hear soft chimes, I hear a ringdove call,
And all the pleasure of the men who played
Reaches me still and keeps me unafraid.

DANCE OF DEATH
(*Air Raid at Norwich*)

The electric lights begin
   To jump as if they'd fuse,
Outside the house a giant dances,
   Pounding in heavy shoes.

A witch astride her broom
   Sweeps on to join the dance—
You hear her sweep as the bombs whizz,
   You hear her broomstick prance.

The windows play a tune,
   Rattling castanets.
Above the town a harpy glides,
   Swoops and pirouettes.

The Dance of Death begins,
   The Witch's Sabbath comes.
The violins already shriek,
   And now begin the drums.

TO THE BLACKBIRD IN MARCH

O Blackbird, try another tune—
You've sung that note for much too long!
You knew quite complicated airs
Last year, and then you perched among
The branches of the flowering pear
Where song-birds ought to be, but now
You poise upon my chimney-pot
As if you really wished to grow
Still blacker from the smuts.   How can
You hope to guard your voice from smoke?
And yet I know that some fine day

I'll wake, as in the past I woke,
To hear that you've remembered all
The music of last year

                       Indeed
The gifted poets, like yourself,
Have chosen smoke and smuts instead
Of ease and cleanness, many times—
Sitting in taverns when they might
Have lived at court, grown rich and sleek,
And carolled for a king's delight.
But all the same, the spring's at hand,
So try at least another tune!
Begin those gay exciting scales
You knew so well, last May and June.

Marguerite Edgelow

ENGLISH PASTORAL

The hill curves down, as smooth as green spun glass
Under blue skies, where little veils of cloud
Like sheerest muslin drift across the height.
A man walks up, leading a great black horse
Who draws a strange machine of painted steel
From which spreads, billowing, a fine white foam
Of lime, to settle gently on the grass.

It might have been a woodcut, rugged, clean,
Aud yet not wan, for blue, green, black and white
Stand sharply out, where each is sunshine-splashed.
What shall we call it—English pastoral?

KATUSHA SPEAKS

*She looks across to the broad, slow-flowing Volga, beyond the
scarred plain, where the tide of battle has recently passed and
fires are still burning. Her pale face is at once beautiful and
inscrutable.*

On burning ground the piled and ruined metal
warps and grows molten under searing pressure,
mingles with bitter breath of wood, dissolving
twin ghosts to ash.

For you are gone, and fallen is the forest;
none may return along that road, none wander
across the pitted earth—earth whose last water
was human blood.

I do not know the way you went, Ilyana,
but that the end is great, needful to Russia
I know.   You will return in the free cornland
to our children.

RED SKY AT MORNING

Softly the moon is glancing
on me, as there it shines
across the tented silence,
the far rock-torn declines.

The sea that has no pulses
frets on the wind-curled sand;
my thoughts are feathers falling
across your sleeping hand.

The mallard in the marshes
stirring the reedy sedge
are watchful for the thrusting
of a new day's molten wedge

And I, alone and quiet,
shall watch the sky from bed
with the tearless eyes of women
who see the day dawn red.

TRIVIAL DETAIL

Floating on the water in the A.R.P. bucket
Was a round reddish speck
That turned out to be a ladybird.
It looked lifeless;
But on a whim
I dipped a finger into the sun-warmed bucket
And extracted the tiny thing.
Laying it on a mellow brick in the rockery,
I went on down the garden path with the bucket
And filled the bird-bath.
And just now, on my way back,
I stopped to look;
And there was the ladybird
Bustling about the hot, richly grooved brick,
Exploring, interested, totally recovered.

I have saved the life of a ladybird!
And, as I refilled the bucket
For its more sinister purpose,
Suddenly, ridiculously,
In the midst of crashing continents,
I felt for a moment
Extraordinarily happy.

Beatrice Gibbs

HERITAGE

What is there here, in these small country places,
    Sleepy and still beneath a cloudy sky,
Where slow men plod, with rain upon their faces,
    That for their keeping none has feared to die?

Green are the meadows, in their patchwork making
    Patterns with fields knee-deep in golden grain
Russet and yellow, ripened for the taking,
    Apples are heavy on the bough again.

Normans have worshipped where the broad grey tower
    Shelters the quiet sleeping of its own,
Cottages cluster, window-sills a-flower,
    Leaning to little paths of cobble-stone.

What is there here, that for its happy living
    Men have not feared to die from age to age?
Beauty that tears the heart, so great its giving,
    England, that is our children's heritage.

THE BOMBER

White moon rising and red sun setting
    White as a searchlight, red as a flame,
Through the dawn wind her hard way making,
    Rhythmless, riddled, the bomber came.

Men who had thought their last flight over,
    All hoping gone, came limping back,
Marvelling, looked on bomb-scarred Dover,
    Buttercup fields and white Down track.

Cottage and ploughland, green lanes weaving,
   Working-folk stopping to stare overhead—
Lovely, most lovely, past all believing
   To eyes of men new-raised from the dead.

KINGFISHER

Here quietly the lazy ripples run,
   Where willows find a mirror at their feet,
The little pool is dappled with the sun,
   And every breath is faint with meadowsweet.
Then suddenly, across the drowsy air
   He darts, a streak of gay exotic light,
The spectrum of the rainbow gathered there,
   A stabbing sword of colour, slim and bright.
And alien to this dreaming muted hour
   One instant on the gentle stream he glints,
Then, glowing brilliant as a tropic flower
   Is gone, a flash of iridescent light.

Now quietly the whispering grasses sigh
For grief that beauty passed so swiftly by.

TROUT

Down by the bridge the speckled trout
   Lie quiet in the pool,
A dragon-fly darts in and out
   The shadows deep and cool.

Out in the Desert, far away,
   I wonder do you dream
Of willow-trees that bend and sway
   Beside a dappled stream:

C

Of quiet hours with rod and line
Casting your chosen fly,
Sad if the weather were too fine,
If fish were small or shy:

Of ripples chilly as they climb
Your waters tall and black,
Of soft green bank for picnic-time,
Of flask and sandwich pack?

Down where the pool is deep and clear
The fat brown trout increase,
Waiting till once again are here
The quiet days of peace.

NIGHT

When all the streets are bright with lamps again
And light streams out from every window-pane,
Then in my heart, each gay and brilliant night,
I shall be thankful for the gift of light.

When but a nightingale sings to the sky,
And only lovers' feet go softly by,
Then in a world the moon and stars possess
I shall be thankful for deep quietness.

When all the danger of the night has gone,
And gently, peacefully, the hours tick on,
Then with true thankfulness my heart will sing,
That night is once again a lovely thing.

WALFORD DAVIES

How jovial was his laughter,
How great his gift to share
The things he loved so simply
With thousands everywhere.
Wide-hearted, wise and gentle,
A good man all his days,
He went his way rejoicing,
His life a song of praise.
Wherever he may travel
This is the certain thing:
The people there will love him,
And he will make them sing.

AT NIGHT

We talked throughout the evening's changing light,
From day gold into pale metallic grey,
And saw the Cézanne cornfield settle for the night
Beneath the moon, cloud swept in disarray.
We leaned upon the window-sill and heard
The flutter of a sudden hurried bird;
The silver coinage on the poplar tree
Shook to the breeze and sounded like the sea.
Our ears shared all the little music then,
Our eyes gazed on the same untroubled view,
But as the passage clock was mumbling ten
I freely left her side and was with you.

SUMMER IN WALES

Lean on the lichen-dappled stone-made wall
    Here in the grassy lane, moor high and calm.
Look on the fields in low lit evening light,
    Their patterned patches gay about the farm.

Blue-green, grey-green, lettuce-green, and emerald,
    A sudden shock of mustard sweeping to the sky,
Ash trees, chestnut, oak, and dark green conifer,
    Hornbeam and copper beech and thorn tree standing
        by.

Grey is the farmhouse, weatherproof and square,
Solid in the pale light, long established there.

Secret are the faces of the men upon the moor;
    Bony and brown are they, hard as a door.
But when they talk to you music is heard,
    For the shepherd speaks with the voice of a bird.

MARCH DAY, 1941

Taut as a tent the heavenly dome is blue,
Uncrossed by cloud or tossing twig or 'plane,
A measureless span infinitely new
To fill the eye and soar the heart again.
Deep in the wintered earth the shock is felt:
Glossy sweet aconite has shown her gold
And string straight crocus spears, where late we knelt
To lodge their bulbs, are waiting to unfold.
The ragged rooks like tea-leaves in the sky
Straggle towards the earth with awkward grace;
A robin in a silver birch nearby
Thrusts up his carol through the naked lace.
    I've known this day for thirty years and more;
    It will go on as it has done before.

THE ELMS ARE FLOWERING

The elms are flowering in a rosy cloud,
A sudden transient blossoming, soon past,
The one fair moment in a stern tree's year
Before its ebon bones are overcast.
High in the fragile feathery branches
Rooks are building thick, untidy nests,
A sooty architecture, old as time,
Beyond the reach of uninvited guests.
Feel the damp wind that lightly passes by;
Smell the damp earth and mark the beaded thorn
That runs above the footpath's narrow cut.
Stand look and sense fulfilment being born.

Blanche Hardy

THE GHOST

The poor ghost stood by the window,
And the room was bright within;
The good-man tired with his labours,
And the housewife settled to spin.
The dogs lay sleeping beside the blaze,
And the children laughed and romped at their plays—
"Oh!" cried Avice, "how the wind blows cold,
God grant the sheep are safe in the fold!"
                "Amen," said the master.

The sad ghost peered through the curtain,
And the room was gay with light;
"An excellent meal," quoth the master,
And the housewife's smile grew bright.
But the old dog sniffed by the fire's side,
And the children stopped, and their eyes grew wide—
"Hark!" cried Avice, "how the wind blows loud!
And look, in the candle—a shroud! a shroud!"
                "Hush, hush," said the mistress.

The good-man laughed and filled his pipe,
And the wind blew fast on the moor;
She crept from the warm hearth-circle
To lift up the latch of the door.
"Oh, my love, is it you that are calling?" she cried;
"Ah rest, for it's soon I'll be there at your side!"
And a breath came out of the whirling night,
And a cold hand fell on her tresses bright—
                "Shut that door," said the master.

THE CHOSEN CHILD

The chosen child must ever be
Misfortunate in his degree;
The loves of earth betray, forsake,
The tired heart is like to break,
The world his grief with scorn regards,
And coldly all his hopes discards:
Their bitter looks let him forget
For midst the stars his way is set.

The distant glory reaches him
Though all the nearer paths be dim,
His feet are torn by rock and brier
His eyes ashine with heavenly fire;
Though limbs be cold and garments thin,
The mystic vision glows within;
From worldly joys his face upturns
To where the immortal spirit burns.

Calamity may cloud his sky,
Riches and honour pass him by,
Lonely he climbs the hills of day,
The shining west gleams far away.
Though armies fall, yet to his eyes
The secret flame shall still arise,
While in his heart as holy ground
The place of peace is ever found.

Ada Jackson

WIDOW-MOTHER

Soldier boy, soldier boy,
    Gallantly you go—
Head erect and shoulders squared,
    Marching heel and toe.

The tale repeats itself, my dear,
    I stood thus, smiling so,
To watch your father marching—five
    And twenty years ago.

And I am proud again.   Again
    A tear comes full and slow.
Can a heart be broken twice?
    Presently I'll know.

There were also some casualties—

BLESSED EVENT

In labour when
the raid began,
she could not run
as others ran.
Now here shall be
no infant's cry,
no navel string
to cut and tie,
she being—by
a bomb well sped—
delivered of
her soul instead.

36

HITLER YOUTH
(*Panzer Division*)

I fell.   Nobody picked me up.
    All day the cars went over me—
The light tanks and the heavy tanks,
    The thunderous artillery.

Now all my bones are powder-fine;
    The stones are grouted with my blood;
I am become the road—the way—
    I thank thee, Fuehrer.   It is good.

All that thou bade me, that I did;
    Gave gladly all I had to give.
Great Fuehrer, let thy will be done—
    But yet I would have liked to live!

I HAVE SEEN ENGLAND

I have seen England
        green with spring
And white with orchards
        blossoming;

England blithe and
        golden-gay
With cowslips on
        an April day;

England beauty—
        garlanded
And crowned with roses
        white and red;

England rich and great
        with sheaves
And yellow fruit
        in tawny leaves;

England folded, field
        and bush
In the hoar-frost's
        dazzling plush.

．　　．　　．

I have seen England
        dark with grief
And red with wounds
        beyond belief;

England grimed
        with battle sweat,
Hard-pressed and grim
        and sore beset

England blackened
        to the bone,
Ringed round with fire,
        betrayed, alone.

But standing with
        her courage whole
Before the frontiers
        of the soul,

Enduring all
        that men may be
Unbound and unafraid
        and free—

．　　．　　．

Two Englands in
        my day have been,
England burning,
        England green;

But God shall show
        a third to me—
England bright
        with victory!

THE MUNITION WORKERS

They sat upon a hill,
They could forget
The dark oppressive roof-tops of the town.
They drank their fill;
The buttercups were wet;
The evening sunlight, webbed and mystical,
Transfused the iron bands that were clamped down
On their bright hair, the fetters of the mill
Became a circlet and a coronet.
The wheels poised and the hammers were laid still.

But now the night is deep,
The caverns burn,
The great machine is grinding in a dream.
They cannot weep,
The coronet is stern,
The fountain of their tears has ceased to gleam:
Somewhere men die; somewhere the waters churn
With flame consumed, somewhere the bullets teem
In this dark night; and wreathe their brows with iron,
With the dread weight of an eternal sleep.

DALLAS: HIS DIRGE

I

Dallas is dead.
It was the tenth of May
When Dallas died,
It was a week ago to-day.

And what is left?
Sylvia.   Sylvia cried
"God! what is left?"
And "Sylvia" the wind replied.
Something of her lay dead at Dallas' side;
She moved and, through a mist of tears,
She saw the vista of the years.
"Dallas is dead"
Said the dawn;
The morning said
"Dallas is gone";
The dreamy afternoon
Whispered "Soon, soon
You will forget!"
But when the sun set
She remembered still,
Her heart was full
Of him, and in the night
She remembered his light.
Remembered he was dead
So that the tears bled
In her eyes
And that her body ached
With an infinity of tears and cries.
I looked at her, I thought "How young you were
"For such a love!" and then "How young you are
To be so sad.   But sorrow has not made you old,
Tragically young indeed the hand I hold,
The hand that Dallas loved!" and the tears poured
On to it, little hand that he adored.
God! he had loved her.   God! she had had his love !
And, now that he was above
And her tears like rain,
I thought "God! you are young enough to start again."

II

I had a Dallas too,
No, he's not dead,
I wish he were, though,
And I've got to make him die,
So that this agony,
This aching lethargy
Of limb, this cry
Of my heart may cease,
And peace
Be mine,
O God divine
Give me peace!
A year ago to-day he sent his love to me,
I laughed a little then,
But soon the laughter grew to be
A laugh of love.   Amen.
He said he'd only lent his love to me,
He came and took it back, and came again
With friendship this time.   I
Prayed God to make him die,
To take away the ghost that haunted me,
That is beloved of me, that drives me mad!
I had
No memories, and I've no youth, no love to give—
No loveliness while Dallas is alive.

FÜHRER

The dead are holy ones and when men die
We reverently hold their memory by
    The sweetest things
    That lent their presence wings
And bound them to us ever tenderly.

And when the giant men, the god-like men,
Each labelled with a miniature of sin
    By those who stand
    And twist an empty hand—
Pass on, they shine in purity again.

Long lies the hammer of the will to wound
Hushed deep, and evil only twines around
    Within its shade.
    And grace is like a blade
That is not pure except its power be found.

But when in darkness like a comet whirled
He dies, no tenderness be there unfurled;
    None shall make dim
    The blood-red light of him
But say he was a man who broke the world.

CONSUMMATUM EST

Light is more beautiful for it is dying,
Peace is more beautiful that doth depart,
Daylight more lovely with the evening
Radiance that blinds the tired heart.

The summer time is richer with more pain
Locked in the white inexorable hold
Of winter, and the lifting of the rain
Is dawn again and wonder to the old.

The dawn of love is stranger than the dawn,
The light of love more shining than the stars,
Yet when the lovers' season was outworn
They only knew the dust of their desires.

ONE GENERATION TO ANOTHER

I shall not die entirely from this earth
    Though even love forget me by and by,
Though all my words become as nothing worth,
    And no man sings my songs; I shall not die.
In after years part of my life will be
    At play about the meadows and the streams,
For I have set my immortality
    Further than songs can go, deeper than dreams.

So, when a child, on some far morn astir
    With April promises, runs in, and spills
Beneath the portrait of his ancestor
    A tumbled heap of meadow daffodils,
He will not know his eyes are bright because
    A child of long ago loved flowers too,
And that strange lady in the picture was
    As pleased as he when April skies were blue.

MARY

When that my Son was born in a little town
    How should I know
His servant, carried on a throne,
    Should through a city go?

And when He turned the bargainers away
    From the long house of prayer,
How should I dream, that in a latter day
    His shrine should find them there.

And in His natal town, for all His words,
    The warring sects increase.
How could I tell there would be heathen guards
    To keep a Christian peace.

TOWN

We have propped ourselves against
    The crowd, and grown afraid
Of wings, and starlight, and the things
    We have not made.

So do we speed the slow blue birth
    Of night with lights, and take
Neat paving-stones to hide the earth
    We could not make.

And since there comes, if silence falls,
    A sudden splash of doubt,
We fashion drums and wheels and walls
    To shut it out.

INTO THE MIDST OF BATTLE

The mountains are at war; flash and flash again
    In the heavy dusk, shower of stone and grass;
The mountains are at war—soldiers from the plain,
    Strange guns in the valley and strange dead in the pass.

Gather in your great-uddered goats,
    The little leaping kids from near and far.
Leave for the first time your fathers' fathers' huts,
    There—the guns again; the mountains are at war
Why should this be, that our earth heaves under us?
    The familiar crag smokes, and the grey cloudy peak
Spits midnight fire, the foot-hills are thunderous;
    O strange brown armies, why do the hills speak?

Fill your coloured pitcher at the spring,
    Pannier the white donkey with its red and blue
        trappings.
It's a long wild journey with a hovel ending;
    The mountains are at war; these are proud happenings.

Here was our land, stubborn and frugal,
    We hoed and harrowed it, scratched at the skin.
Your mines go deeper, but the wounds are unfruitful.
    The mountains are at war, but the mountains win.

Make fast the spurred legs of the speckled cock,
    Go down the cattle track, your lean dogs about you,
With your children and your goods; the mountains rock,
    They are possessed of soldiers and are best without
        you.

But, going, still remember the peace of goat bells,
    A stream falling, the loneliness of stars,
The impervious seasons creeping on the hills
    That were before and shall endure beyond all wars.

Sylvia Lynd

R.A.F., MAY, 1940

I heard the squadron flying home
At midnight high among the stars;
Never did tale of Greece or Rome
Tell of such heroes or such wars.

Legend nor boast nor history
Proclaims such deeds as these achieve,
Who daily fight Thermopylae,
Who snatch the glove from Death, and live.

Perseus and Bellerophon,
They, too, were fighters and had wings,
They fought with monsters and they won,
And in the stars their glory rings.

Castor and Pollux keep their station,
Neither do we dispute their claim
If a more glorious constellation
Should mark a still more glorious fame.

Instead of Bear, or Wain, or Plough,
Splendid to see in night's great dome,
Give to those stars a new name now,
Call them the Squadron Flying Home.

THE FLYCATCHER

That is the flycatcher's wing beneath the eaves,
A frivolous quick sound like an opening fan.
Under the scalloped canopy of leaves

He has found the nest made in some other Spring
Between the wall and the tall creeper stem,
Old as the wall itself, a slender tree
(Perhaps one of Raleigh's earliest transplanting);
And now about the window flit from earliest dawn
The skilful wings.   A bird of urbane
Elegance is the flycatcher, straight backed, self possessed,
    slim.
He watches and marks his prey and neatly outflies him,
A peregrine in miniature.   The midges are conspicu-
    ously
Fewer for his hunting.
Good luck, it is said, attends the dwelling that he makes
    his own.
Certain it is, when he is gone, Summer is gone.

Viola Meynell

THE BLIND MAN'S MORNING

Sleeping he is not blind
More than another.
But dawn's faint wind,
Blowing rosy light,
Whispers: "Rise brother,
To thy night."

DAWN'S FIRST VOICE

I awoke—perhaps too late?
The greying window said, Wait.
Then, O my herald, you stirred
And spoke—spoke once, and then sang,
The day's first sweet sweet bird;
To this one place it was given,
And I was the one who heard.

I may think it so if I will!
But in the next field, and next still,
In each village a first bird wakes,
In each lane throughout the land
A first bird stirs and makes
Morning from night, with a hint
Of hope to a heart that breaks.

TO THE WOMEN OF EUROPE

Sometimes, between the fighting and the crying,
    Between the long wars and the short-lived peace,
We hear, beyond ourselves, a sweet, clear music—
    And then the battles and the weeping cease.

For, misted by our thought, dimmed by our seeing,
    But known complete, whole, beautiful and true,
Its walls and spires a fountaining of music,
    Our native city beacons on the view.

Real, for we build it; lovely with our longing;
    Shining, no dream, down vistas of the mind:
Our hands are lit, and vision-lit our pathway,
    "Seek," said the Master, "Seek, and ye *shall* find."

THE TOKEN

I passed along a tragic street,
Trod broken glass beneath my feet,
Saw ribs of roof, and drifting doors,
And ceilings crashed on splintered floors.
Dear treasured 'sticks' of beds and chairs
Streamed like a flood down lonely stairs;
The tender, slow-grown flesh of Home
Gaped from its shattered structural bone.
Can Time and Patience build again
Love's complex form, here lying slain?
I asked, and sighed, and turned away;
Then saw, against the setting day,
A birch tree lean its rose-gilt head
Above the pitiful ugly dead,
So lovely, so serene, secure,
Whispering that Beauty does endure.

49

Ruth Pitter

THE SPARROW'S SKULL
Memento mori
Written at the Fall of France

The kingdoms fall in sequence, like the waves on the
    shore.
All save divine and desperate hopes go down, they are
    no more:
Solitary is our place, the castle in the sea,
And I muse on those I have loved, and on those who
    have loved me.

I gather up my loves, and keep them all warm,
While above our heads blows the bitter storm:
The blessed natural loves, of life-supporting flame,
And those whose name is Wonder, which have no other
    name.

The skull is in my hand, the minute cup of bone,
And I remember her, the tame, the loving one,
Who came in at the window, and seemed to have a mind
More towards sorrowful man than to those of her own
    kind.

She came for a long time, but at length she grew old;
And on her death-day she came, so feeble and so bold;
And all day, as if knowing what the day would bring,
She waited by the window, with her head beneath her
    wing.

And I will keep the skull, for in the hollow here
Lodged the minute brain that had outgrown a fear;
Transcended an old terror, and found a new love,
And entered a strange life, a world it was not of.

Even so, dread God! even so, my Lord!
The fire is at my feet, and at my breast the sword,
And I must gather up my soul, and clap my wings, and
        flee
Into the heart of terror, to find myself in Thee.

SEAGULLS IN LONDON, JANUARY, 1940

They stormed upon me like catastrophe.
All fear of man was gone: scenting the food,
The harpy-crowd gathered and broke on me.
These, bred in solitude
Among the sea-pink in the salt sea-marsh,
Moated about by creeks of quaking slime
Lonelier than mountain deserts, now with harsh
Throats besought alms at this most bitter time.

My hands, cold-palsied, felt their crooked bills,
Their pirate sails struck on my stiffened cheek;
Their cold wet feet touched me with fleeting chills
Frail and inadvertent, that seemed to speak
For all the fury, of existence weak;
And one was lame,
Lagged on the turn, got nothing when he came.

Heart-withering hunger! how the terror whips
The shrinking mind! knowing ourselves curtailed,
More steel, less grain loading the threatened ships,
We, for whom plenty never yet has failed,
Feel the frore shadow of what famine now
Clutches the bowels of both foe and friend,
And while all Europe shudders in the snow
Dare not foresee, nor think upon the end.

And I am moved to ask you to forgive
If I have hope: if like a stubborn seed

The heart turns tough, determined still to live,
Made a mere dormant centre of the need
For bare existence, of the will to be:
If this is hardness, O forgive it me!

Pardon the faith, that will not be denied,
One with my life, and needing not a name,
That like these wings over the rushing tide
Beats upward, and not knowing whence it came
Battles with *hunger, anguish, and the sea*!
If this be folly, O forgive it me!

YOUR GARDEN

The violets are here to be picked,
Your violets,
Large and purple and smelling sweet,
And the aconites have come out
Beneath the trees,
Your aconites.
In the southern border under the wall
Are delicate iris stylosa, filmy and fragrant,
Your irises.
O gentle, lovely spirit that tended these flowers,
Where are you?
You cannot have left all these that were a part of you.
Are you mingled with them,
A fragrance?
A breath?

BUCKINGHAMSHIRE PLACE NAMES

Go take the Upper Icknield Way
Through Wendover and roam
Across the Chilterns to the woods
Of Hampden's ancient home.

There's Stokenchurch and Stewkley,
High Wycombe, Slough and Penn,
Stoke Mandeville, and Fingest
Beech hidden in a glen.

There's Amersham and Aylesbury
And Beaconsfield, Coleshill,
There's Burnham, Wing, and Olney
Where lace is made with skill.

Between the Chalfonts, Peter, Giles,
And on past Shardeloes,
The little Misbourne winds and curves,
From Missenden it flows.

On Bledlow Ridge the wind blows soft
Across the Vale to Brill;
And guarding Hughenden there spreads
The common of Naphill.

. . . .

Such are the names that fall from local lips,
Telling of British, Saxon, Norman times,
Precious inheritance from our forgotten past,
Sweet to the ear as are old ballad rhymes.

AT THE NATIONAL GALLERY CONCERTS

They come as to a shrine,
Eager, expectant,
Wave upon wave of pilgrims seeking rest—
Rest from the cares of war;
Exiles there are, and those once persecuted.
And as the music floats from lofty dome
The listening crowd is one—
One soul set free.
Pity and love flow through them with sweet force;
Wisdom, forbearance, hope surge in their hearts,
And courage triumphs over all dismay!

MAGNOLIA

Exotic stranger, whose most costly scent
Might, with sweet odour, flood a Continent;
Whose opulent voluptuousness looks down
Amazed upon an English country town,
(So Messalina, exiled, might we see
Brooding, astonished, at a parish tea);
What do you here, lost Empress?—How old
Our sun must seem, our warmest winds, how cold!
What thoughts are yours?   Those petals of thick cream
Lie lapped and laved in a continuous dream
Of forests, dark as death, yet shining bright
With Tropic blooms, all insolence and might,
Which poison with hot breath the violent air;
Their frantic perfume heavy like despair!—
What vision haunts your discontented hours,
Proudest and most disdainful of all flowers?
Alas! no gorgeous butterfly arrayed
In million colours may your charms invade,
Nor warrior insect, from green swamp upstrung,
Taste your strong honey with his dart-like tongue;
Only domestic bees, and drowsy, small
Provincial insects sometimes dare to call,
Then flee from such rich banquetings, oppressed
By foreign flavours which they deem unblessed.—
Magnolia, in your petals, every one,
You hold delights which we, suspicious, shun.—
Let those who would not in such secrets share,
Of your dramatic loveliness beware!

NEGLECTED WOODS

Neglected woods, all overgrown,
Now, have you come into your own!—
Like children from an infant school,
Rush out wild fronds which know no rule:
Briars across the footpath spread,
Confuse my hesitating tread.
Stark Revolution here I see
Deriding man's weak mastery.—
I love you thus, rebellious Wood,
Though I lie prone where once I stood,
As we trap creatures, trapped, in turn,
By unsubdued, defiant fern.
Your trees are into tyrants grown;
I, a meek slave, salute your throne.
Should I offend, what doom might fall
On me, alone, amongst you all,
What execution dealt to me
By the rough justice of a Tree?—
Grant me your Freedom, Woods, and give
Me, in your shade, the right to live.
Surely, a Poet should fare well
As bird, within your citadel.
Scarring his untamed heart you'll find
Tracks, like your own, which turn and wind
Purposeless, all crissed and crossed
Clear at first then quickly lost.
Brambles, too, and elfin, queer
Mushroom growth do flourish there.
And leaves (ah, leaves!) the winds whirled down
Ere he could weave them in a crown—
Therefore, Woods, be kind, be kind
To a creature of like mind,
Grant, even as to a mouse or vole
Green shelters to an errant soul!

V. Sackville-West

FRITILLARIES
(From *The Land*)

But once I went through the lanes, over the sharp
Tilt of the little bridges; past the forge,
And heard the clang of anvil and iron,
And saw the founting sparks in the dusky forge,
And men outside with horses, gossiping.
So I came through that April England, moist
And green in its lush fields between the willows,
Foaming with cherry in the woods, and pale
With clouds of lady's-smock along the hedge,
Until I came to a gate and left the road
For the gentle fields that enticed me, by the farms,
Wandering through the embroidered fields, each one
So like its fellow; wandered through the gaps,
Past the mild cattle knee-deep in the brooks,
And wandered drowsing as the meadows drowsed
Under the pale wide heaven and slow clouds.
And then I came to a field where the springing grass
Was dulled by the hanging cups of fritillaries,
Sullen and foreign-looking, the snaky flower,
Scarfed in dull purple, like Egyptian girls
Camping among the furze, staining the waste
With foreign colour, sulky—dark and quaint,
Dangerous too, as a girl might sidle up,
An Egyptian girl, with an ancient snaring spell,
Throwing a net, soft round the limbs and heart,
Captivity soft and abhorrent, a close-meshed net,
—See the square web on the murrey flesh of the flower—
Holding her captive close with her bare brown arms.
Close to her little breast beneath the silk,

A gipsy Judith, witch of a ragged tent,
And I sank from the English field of fritillaries
Before it should be too late, before I forgot
The cherry white in the woods, and the curdled clouds,
And the lapwings crying free above the plough.

Mary Doreen Spender

FOR RICHARD SPENDER

Gone in an instant
Like a light, when fingers touch the switch,
In the last second of his consciousness,
Leading his men in Tunis.
Gone, like the light.
And yet, not like the light.   He suffered and he sang.
And in his growth he rooted in our hearts,
Until he seems the fabric of our lives.
So in the Spring we stand, our eyes still gazing,
For all the thousand tints of green and myriad flowers
Seem just for him—not wreaths spread on a grave,
But little brother buds that blow and glow beside him.
Our ears, too, listen to the song of birds,
Which fall felicitous from green hedge and tree,
Voices as sweet and piercing as his own.

That grey-haired age should weep with mordant sorrow
For lovely golden youth in glorious Spring,
—A sad reversal of accustomed ways!
And yet—who knows?
A comet on the low horizon
Shines in the dark before the break of day.
A mystery to us, what path it follows hidden,
And what, beyond our sight, its secret orbit shows.

NIGHT ON DARTMOOR

Dark—and a still night, lying up here on Dartmoor
Cheek to the moorland grasses, dreaming awake in the
blackness,

Long-left houses of men and their graves and temples
    I know as stones on the torside.
Not a bird is awake. And no beast moves in the
    brambles.
What can be here, in this land of ling and bracken,
Which calls and calls through the hovering clouds of the
    hill-mist
    And mists of the long forgotten?
Hark! Far away is sounding and beating a measure.
—Not the grey river, though that, too, sounds in the
    valley—
Beating! A tiny drum in the darkness,
And far, far off the note of a horn is calling!

    Yes, it's a measure for dancing feet,
        Light, and far in some hollow,
    Distant and tiny, unearthly sweet,
        Shall I arise and follow?

    They must be dancing over the rise
        Who is playing the measure?
    Glistening colours of what strange dyes,
        Brightness and airy pleasure!

    Clear comes the call of the music's beat,
        And a harper's notes are ringing,
    A fiddle keeps time for the dancers' feet
        And a wordless voice is singing.

    Sweeter and brighter than moon or sun
        Must be the lights and the faces.
    I go to join the fairy fun,
        With the dancers in their places.

    .   .   .   .   .

Dark—and a still night, standing up here on Dartmoor.
Only the river babbles, far down there in the valley—
I know there are homes and graves of the long-
     forgotten—
But, ah! no lights—no harp sounds over the grasses!
Gone! Beautiful wordless voice, and feet of the far off
     dancers.

Margaret Stanley-Wrench

LEGACY

Long after it will happen, when all is forgotten,
That somewhere a woman walking into a greenhouse
In the dusty haze of noon when thought is suspended,
Will stop, fear like a finger on her heart
At the sound of a bee trapped beneath the glass.

Others whom the casual accident
Of clear skies and falling leaves and the smell
Of rain and woodfires and the hollow song of birds
Reminds the heart of what it should forget,
Of days and voices that will not come again;

Or who, at the lonely sound of trains at night
Will turn restlessly to shut out thought,
Or whose hearts will clench with fear at the whine of a
   wheel
On wet roads. And some will not endure
The aimless sound of the relentless sea.

AUTUMN ROSES

Now when the year dips swiftly towards winter
And the sun slants steeply, and the mild afternoons
Are yellow as apples mellowing on the tree,
The roses flower again, now with the threat
Of frost and fall and dissolution of rain
Like blight for the last blooming. Clearer now
As if the frost shone through them, sweet with all
The summer's sun and all the summer's rain

Sucked into a brief glow, as if that light
Had now a form and shape and was a rose
Curled thin as a shell and smooth as wax to the finger,
And brighter now than when the haze of June
Throbbed like a string with heat and life and movement.

In this warm pause before the death of winter
Has seized the heart, as frost blackens the flower,
All loveliness halts on its height of beauty,
The butterfly that opens like a rose
Gratefully in the ripeness of the sun,
The rose with a heart clotted with threads of gold,
The fruit that breaks in sweetness on the ground
Before the rot, the mildew and the fog
Corrupt the yellow and the glowing leaf,
As, in the evening, before the light has gone
All light is brighter, as if through the fragile skin
Of the sky some other light like fire is pressing
Before the even greyness of the night.

PLOUGHING UP THE PASTURE

Now up the pasture's slope the ploughed land laps
In folds that fall and crumble from the share,
Rooks dip to the warm earth, hot leather creaks,
The sweat of labouring flesh steams in the air,
The flanks of beasts are smooth with sun and toil,
The cropped turves that are worn with years of grazing
Turn inwards to the steel, and over the long
Acres of grassland stretch the ribs of soil.
No longer when in summer the clotted shadows
Fall from the crest of trees, will they stretch over
The lazy turf, but will shadow a new world
Of yellow acres, fret and stir of meadows,
Green barley, freckled silver by the wind.
And corn like a fresh sea across the wold.

Louise Stewart

THE SEA-WOLF

The brown boats are sailing the wide seas tonight,
Looking doon is the moon wi' her deid face sae white,
The rim o' the sky is a' reddened wi' tears,
And the sea-mews are making a dirge o' their fears.

The wind's pipes are skirling "Lochaber no More",
Oh! it's wae for the ones that are left on the shore;
Their hearts—like the sea's heart—are loupin' wi' fright,
Looking doon is the moon wi' her deid face sae white.

Far, far are the bonnie brown boats frae the bay,
Cauld guests noo o' darkness and danger are they;
The Night Pack is hunting the lads' lives again—
Frae ruth o' the Sea-Wolf, Dear God, bield oor men.

Marie Carmichael Stopes

Extracts from "Instead of Tears"
In Memoriam of H.M.S. Cossack
(*And especially for Lieut. H. William Rose, R.N.*)

Our grief for you, poignant, and personal
But crystallizes woe for all our dead
In this foul war, that sprang upon the mind
Like nightmare fiend upon the sleeping man,
Whose head was pillowed on fair dreaming peace.
In secret, Evil sharped his horrid claws
To rend in tatters ancient free men's laws,
To shackle for all time with no release
Nations who marched in freedom's gallant van.
You were on guard, you and your noble kind
To take the blows on your symbolic head:
We owe to you a song-wreathed pedestal.

Mothers of sons who that same day went down
May pride sustain you when your hearts are sore,
Pride that you mothered men who leaping, said
"The Navy's here" as *Cossack* grappled to
In line with Drake.   Last visions of the brave
Upon a sinking deck must be your pride
Wherein your tears, your grief, not they, have died.
Your sons spring forward from their watery grave
To hold our ships that they may win straight through
The darkest night.   Immortalized though dead
In this world you will meet your sons no more:
Think of the thorns upon the Saviour's crown.

I must go to the garden's flower-stocked bed
Where you had planned to dig the scented earth

That muscles should be gently harnessed in
  To spirits' service, and from soil to draw
    Soul's nutriment with body's nourishment.
    When of all outward clamour I am rid
    In quiet gardens I will softly bid
    The lily fill her cup with scented thought
    To fling abroad your purest dreams of law
  For all mankind, to close the road to sin.
Winds from the sea repeat, repeat, give birth
To echoes that your gospel may be spread.

  · · · · ·

We your true friends who loved your radiant glow
  Rippling with laughter, reaching out from strength,
    Who loved your hands grappling with urgent work
    Your eager eyes, piercing the distant light
    Your beating heart, firm in its tenderness,
      Your upright will to serve our country's need,
        The bell of your great voice, its power to plead
      With a contagious valiant happiness;
    You were a magnet drawing towards the right
    Those who, alone, life's harder tasks would shirk;
We had not known to what a bitter length
Our salt tears on salt waves for you would flow.

  · · · · ·

You stepped through matter, but you have not gone
  Your imprint on too many hearts was set
    For you to vanish like a morning cloud;
      True love in motion cannot thus be checked.
      As the Immortals fought upon the plain
        With power enhanced by spirits freer guise
          Unfurl new wings of love across our skies.
        Like Homer's heroes, fight for us again.
      What happens when a gallant ship is wrecked
    And moving water is her winding-shroud?
  In seeming chaos life does not forget.
You stepped through matter, sweep our spirits on!

THE LIFT DESCENDING

The lift descending took my love from me.
My heart pretending there was naught to see,
Looked up.   O there!   Between smooth metal bars
Your eyes shone, sudden cloud-enveloped stars.
Your firm lips melted and your face was set
With look so piercing I remember yet
The sweet stir of its entry to my heart,
The long, slow torture as we drew apart,
The tension intimate of tendons stretched
To breaking point, as downwards I was fetched.
Where my heart had been, now a wound was gaping
And all time stopped, though space was still escaping.

O. I. *Ward*

SONG OF A SEABOOT STOCKING

Knit, knit, knit, in the watches of the night,
Plain, purl, plain, purl, beneath a dim blue light;
With Dorniers droning overhead and crashing guns
    below,
A seaboot stocking lengthens out, row upon weary row.

Knit, knit, knit, in shelters all day long;
The stocking's getting dirty, the pattern's going wrong,
The oiled wool slithers off the pins, the stitches dis-
    appear
As I hastily retrieve them, just in time for the All Clear.

Knit, knit, knit, in London's Underground;
The snores are rising from the bunks, the cocoa's coming
    round;
The last train has just rumbled through, the shelterers
    shake down
While overhead the Fire Guard keep their watch o'er
    London Town.

FRAGMENT

I know that life could be like poetry;
Were you to share it with me and inspire
Warm ecstasy, swift beauty and desire,
How great the glory in each passing day!
And though our joy be fashioned of stern things,
Snatched opportunities and fleeting dreams,
Yet so our unity should be complete,
Miraculous and infinite our lot,
For understanding must give strength in strife,
Ah, God, if dear Reality should breathe
Her promise on this soul of mine that longs
To give, and never to withhold the love
That springs in bright confusion and sublime
To lose itself in your heart for all time!

Dorothy Wellesley

THE BURIED CHILD

He is not dead, nor liveth
The little child in the grave;
And men have known for ever
That he walketh again:
They hear him November evenings,
When acorns fall with the rain.

Deep in the hearts of men
Within his tomb he lieth,
And when the heart is desolate
He desolate sigheth.

Teach me, then, the heart of the dead child,
Who, holding a tulip, goeth
Up the stairs in his little grave-shift,
Sitting down in his little chair
By his biscuit and orange,
In the nursery he knoweth.

Teach me all that the child, who knew life
And the quiet of death,
To the croon of the cradle-song
By his brother's crib,
In the deeps of the nursery dusk
To his mother saith.

REUNION

When the red embers on the hearth glow bright,
And the snow-muffled world in silence lies;
When wrapped in dreams so wrought with mysteries
The sleeping scarce draw breath, I take my flight
Out through the shadow, out, out into the night,
The deep, broad night encompassing the skies
With filaments of silver, where, full of eyes,
The heavens swing, a galaxy of light.

Gone is the close shut room; the lingering fire
Holds for me now no comfort, though the heat
Glows kindly on my body in its chair.
My spirit wings in fullness of desire
Up through the starry aisles my love to meet,
And I am free of earth, and earth's despair.

TO SAINT FRANCIS OF ASSISI
October 4th, 1943

You walked the fields of Italy
Your naked feet with peace were shod;
You carried wild flowers in your hands
And in your heart you carried God.

Your bed was tangled leaves and grass,
At times a thorn would pierce your side;
And with you for companion
Walked Poverty, your Lady-Bride.

Through the wide golden Umbrian plains
You sought the Timeless and the Still,
And in your timeless, mystic world
You found and loved the Perfect Will . . .

Come back great Saint to Italy
Your land to-day in ashes lies;
Not ashes of humility
That claimed you 'neath Assisian skies.

Ashes of lust and greed and hate
A traitor-hand to-day has flung
About your paths, and where you sang
Your canticles a dirge is sung.

Come back O Little Saint of Love
With Holy Michael wield the sword
Of God, till Satan be cast down
To hell; till reigns the Living Word—

Come, Francis of the burning heart
The burning feet, the burning hand;
Burn clean through sacrificial fires
Your own incomparable land.

IMMORTALITY

Now you are dead, though summer brings
Her beauty and her waywardness,
Shall all her music pleasure me
As one soft rustle of your dress?

Now you are dead, and roses vie
In whiteness with your folded calm,
Shall this pale peace encircle me
As the warm wonder of your arm?

You are not dead.   What foolishness!
Though fast the grave your body keep,
The gracious, live, essential you
Shall steal upon my lonely sleep—

And we shall walk new mystic ways
Together, and this pain shall pass
Quietly, as now your grave-flowers fall
To mingle with the living grass.

HEAVEN

Heaven shines over the mountains,
Earth with its glory pales;
Love is of love begotten—
And sweet is the print of the Nails.

He came through the fragrant morning,
Treading the day new-born.
Light is of Light begotten—
And sweet is the mark of the Thorn.

Down He came to the city,
To the city tortured and drear.
Peace is of Peace begotten—
And deep is the Wound of the Spear . . .

Of Nails and Spear and Thorn-wood
Are a Shield and a Shelter made.
Home is of Home begotten—
And for all is a Table laid.

Heaven shines over the city,
Blood is the Vintage shed;
Life is of Life begotten
And sweet is Our Daily Bread.

DAVID

Why should the gay, the beautiful, the young
Go forth to fight the battles of the old,
Whose hearts grown disillusioned, dumb and cold
Have long since, dying songs of freedom sung
To the last word; and from whose harps unstrung
Dead lilies fall to mingle with the mould?
Only reflected fires can make these bold
With sacrificial ardours of the tongue:—

'In Singapore my son fell.' 'India
Holds my Beloved, slain on the wild North-West.'
'And mine lies buried 'neath dark domes of ice.'
'Deep in the desert sands of Syria
My grandson sleeps.' 'Is this the devil's jest?'
'*Not David—but Goliath paid the price.*'

Margaret L. Woods

MARCH THOUGHTS FROM ENGLAND

O that I were lying under the olives,
Lying alone among the anemones!
Shell-coloured blossoms they bloom there and scarlet,
Far under stretches of silver woodland,
Flame in the delicate shade of the olives.
O that I were lying under the olives!
Grey grows the thyme on the shadowless headland,
The long low headland, where white in the sunshine,
The rocks run seaward.   It seems suspended
Lone in an infinite gulf of azure.

There were I lying under the olives,
Might I behold come following seaward,
Clear brown shapes in a world of sunshine,
A russet shepherd, his sheep too, russet.
Watch them wander the long grey headland
Out to the end of the burning azure.

O that I were lying under the olives!
So should I see the far-off cities
Glittering low by the purple water,
Gleaming high on the purple mountain;
See where the road goes winding southward.
It passes the valleys of almond blossom,
Curves round the crag o'er the steep-hanging orchards,
Where almond and peach are aflush 'mid the olives—
Hardly the amethyst sea shines through them—
Over it cypress on solemn cypress
Lead to the lonely pilgrimage places.

O that I were dreaming under the olives!
Hearing alone on a sun-steeped headland
A crystalline wave, almost inaudible,
Steal round the shore; and thin, far off,
The shepherd's music.   So did it sound
In fields Sicilian, Theocritus heard it,
Moschus and Bion piped it at noontide.

O that I were listening under the olives!
So should I hear behind in the woodland
The peasants talking.   Either a woman,
A wrinkled grandame, stands in the sunshine,
Stirs the brown soil in an acre of violets—
Large odorous violets—and answers slowly
A child's swift babble; or else at noon
The labourers come.   They rest in the shadow,
Eating their dinner of herbs, and are merry.

Soft speech Provençal under the olives!
Like a queen's raiment from days long perished,
Breathing aromas of old unremembered
Perfumes and shining in dust-covered places
With sudden hints of forgotten splendour—
So on the lips of the peasant his language,
His only now, the tongue of the peasant.

Would I were listening under the olives!
So should I see in an airy pageant
A proud chivalrous pomp sweep by me,
Hear in high courts the joyous ladies
Devising of Love in a world of lovers:
Hear the song of the Lion-hearted,
A deep-voiced song—and oh! perchance,
Ghostly and strange and sweet to madness,
Rudel sing the Lady of Tripoli.

MADE AND PRINTED IN GREAT BRITAIN BY THE ANCHOR PRESS, LTD., TIPTREE, ESSEX